# *Food*
# RICE

Louise Spilsbury

Heinemann
LIBRARY

www.heinemann.co.uk/library
Visit our website to find out more information about Heinemann Library books.

To order:
☎ Phone 44 (0) 1865 888066
📄 Send a fax to 44 (0) 1865 314091
💻 Visit the Heinemann Bookshop at www.heinemann.co.uk/library to browse our catalogue and order online.

First published in Great Britain by Heinemann Library,
Halley Court, Jordan Hill, Oxford OX2 8EJ
a division of Reed Educational and Professional Publishing Ltd.
Heinemann is a registered trademark of Reed Educational & Professional Publishing Ltd.

OXFORD  MELBOURNE  AUCKLAND
JOHANNESBURG  BLANTYRE  GABORONE
IBADAN  PORTSMOUTH (NH)  USA  CHICAGO

Designed by Celia Floyd
Illustrated by Barry Atkinson
Originated by Ambassador Litho Ltd
Printed by South China Printing Co in Hong Kong.

ISBN 0 431 12705 0
05 04 03 02 01
10 9 8 7 6 5 4 3 2 1

**British Library Cataloguing in Publication Data**
Splisbury, Louise
    Rice. – (Food)
    1. Rice  2. Cookery (Rice)
    I. Title
    641.3'318

**Acknowledgements**
The Publishers would like to thank the following for permission to reproduce photographs:
Anthony Blake Photo Library pp.9, 12, 15, 20; Corbis /Tony Arruza pp.11, 19, /Patrick Bennett p.17, /Owen Franken p.10, /Philip Gould p.21, /Becky Luigart-Stayner p.6, /The Purcell Team p.14; Gareth Boden pp.7, 23, 24, 25, 28, 29; Heather Angel p.16; Photodisc pp.5, /Jackson Vereen/Cole Group p.22; Tony Stone /Gary John Norman p.18, /John Midgley p.8; Trip/W. Jacobs p.4.

Cover photograph reproduced with permission of Photodisc.

Every effort has been made to contact copyright holders of any material reproduced in this book. Any omissions will be rectified in subsequent printings if notice is given to the Publisher.

# CONTENTS

Words written in bold, **like this**, are explained in the Glossary.

# WHAT IS RICE?

Rice is a very important food for more than half the people in the world. Many people in **Asia** eat rice two or three times a day.

Rice is a **cereal**. It is part of the grass **family**. The rice grains we eat are the **seeds** of the rice plant.

rice seeds

# KINDS OF RICE

There are two main kinds of rice – long **grain** and short grain. Short grain rice is sticky when cooked. In Italy, people use it to make a dish called risotto.

Long grain rice cooks into separate grains. Lots of Indian food is made from long grain rice, including this spicy rice dish called pilau.

# IN THE PAST

People in **Asia** have grown and eaten rice for 5000 years. Farmers in Bali probably first built these **terraces** to grow rice over 2000 years ago.

In some places rice was stored in special barns. People built these to keep the rice **gods** happy. They believed the rice gods would help them grow lots of rice.

# AROUND THE WORLD

In **Asian** countries local people eat most of the rice they grow. Farmers sell any extra rice to local companies.

A lot of rice is also grown in America and Australia. Most of this rice is **exported**. This means it is taken to other countries to be sold.

# LOOKING AT RICE

The **stalk** of the rice plant is hollow like a straw. It soaks up water from the **roots**, which are planted in water. The **spikelets** at the top of the plant contain the rice **grains**.

spikelets

stalk

Brown rice is the grain after the outer **husk** has been removed. For white rice the outer **bran** layers are also taken off. This is a rice grain.

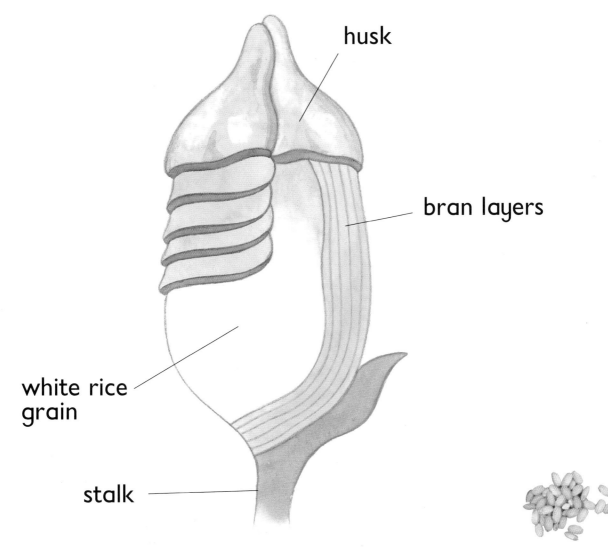

husk

bran layers

white rice grain

stalk

# PLANTING RICE

In most parts of **Asia**, rice **seeds** are planted in special **seed beds**. Then the young plants are re-planted by hand into the rice fields or **terraces**.

In America and Australia, aeroplanes carry rice seeds and drop them as they fly over the farmers' fields.

# HOW RICE GROWS

Rice plants grow best when their **roots** are under water. In many **Asian** countries **monsoon** rains fill the rice fields. Mud walls keep the water in.

In countries like America and Australia, there are few long spells of rainfall. Machines pump water into the rice fields to help the rice grow.

# WHAT HAPPENS NEXT?

When the rice is ready, the water is let out of the rice fields. Some farmers cut the rice plants by hand. Then they beat the **stalks** to shake off the **grain**.

In other places machines do the work. Giant **combine harvesters** cut down the plants. They also separate the grain from the stalks.

# RICE TO EAT

After drying the **grains** in the sun, some farmers crush them to loosen their hard **husks**. Then they toss the grains in the air to get the loose husks off.

In some places machines with big rollers rub the grains to make the husks come off. For white rice the **bran** layer is taken off by rubbing the grains roughly together in a machine.

# EATING RICE

People eat rice in many different ways. You can eat it hot or cold, in cakes and puddings, on its own or with meat or vegetables. In Japan, rice is used to make dishes like these sushi.

Rice is also used to make other kinds of food. Special machines make a popular breakfast food by puffing up rice **grains**.

# GOOD FOR YOU

Rice is a **carbohydrate**. This means it is a kind of food that gives us **energy**. We need energy for everything we do.

Brown rice is better for you than white rice. The **bran** layer contains **vitamins** and **fibre**. These **nutrients** help to keep you healthy.

# HEALTHY EATING

You need to eat different kinds of food to keep well. This food pyramid shows how much of each different food you need.

Rice is in the group of foods at the bottom of the pyramid. You need to eat some of the things in that group every day. In fact, you can eat a food from this group at every meal.

You should eat some of the foods shown in the middle every day, too. You need only small amounts of the foods at the top.

The food in each part of the pyramid helps your body in different ways.

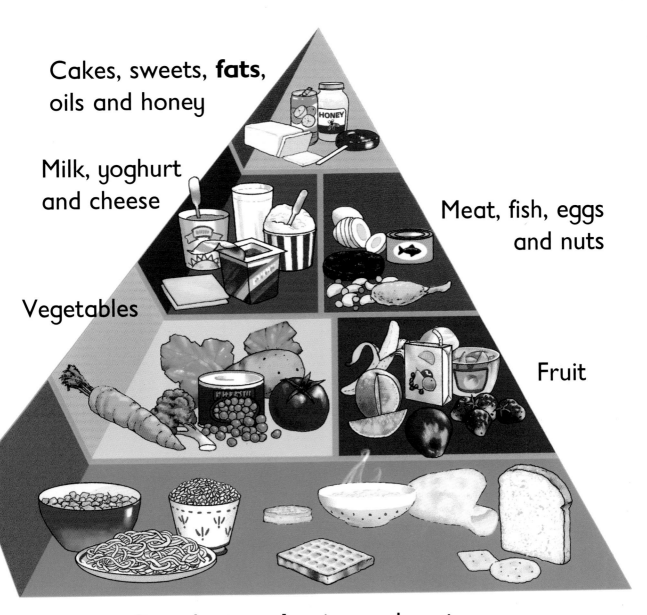

Cakes, sweets, **fats**, oils and honey

Milk, yoghurt and cheese

Meat, fish, eggs and nuts

Vegetables

Fruit

Bread, **cereals**, rice and pasta

27

# RICE PUDDING RECIPE

1 Rub the butter around a shallow oven dish.

2 Add the short **grain** pudding rice.

**You will need:**
- a little butter
- 25g short grain pudding rice
- 600 ml milk
- 50g sugar

Ask an adult to help you!

3  Stir in the milk and sugar.

4  Bake in the oven for $2\frac{1}{2}$ to 3 hours at 170°C/325°F/Gas Mark 3.

# GLOSSARY

**Asia** part of the world made up of different countries, including China, Japan, Thailand and India. Asian means people or things from Asia.

**bran** thin brown layer between the husk and the seed of a cereal plant

**carbohydrates** goodness from the food we eat that gives us energy

**cereal** grains like wheat and rice that are used to make flour, bread and breakfast foods

**combine harvester** farm machine that cuts cereal plants like rice, and separates the grain from the stalks

**energy** all living things need energy to live, move and grow. Our energy comes from our food.

**exported** when a product is made in one country but taken to another country to be sold

**family** group of plants or animals that are alike

**fats** nutrients found in some foods. Butter, oil and margarine are kinds of fat.

**fibre** part of a plant that passes through our bodies when we eat it. As it does this it helps to keep our bodies healthy.

30

**gods**   beings believed to have great power over human lives

**grain**   seed of a cereal plant

**husk**   dry outer covering of a seed

**monsoon**   most countries in Asia have three seasons – one dry, one rainy and one cold. The monsoon is the rainy season.

**nutrient**   the goodness in food we need to stay healthy

**roots**   plant parts that grow down into soil. They take in water and nutrients from the soil.

**seeds**   made by the plant and released to grow into new plants

**seed beds**   special areas of fine soil where seeds are planted closely together until they become young plants (seedlings)

**spikelets**   part of the flowering top of the plant that holds the seeds

**stalk**   part of the plant that holds the leaves and flowers up above the ground

**terraces**   flat areas on a slope that are used for farming. They look like giant steps on the sides of a hill.

**vitamins**   group of nutrients that keep your body healthy and help you grow

# MORE BOOKS TO READ

*Senses: Tasting*, K. Hartley, C. Macro, P. Taylor, Heinemann Library, 2000

*Plants: How Plants Grow*, Angela Royston, Heinemann Library, 1999

*Safe and Sound: Eat Well*, Angela Royston, Heinemann Library, 1999

*A Visit to China*, Peter & Connie Roop, Heinemann Library, 1998

*What's for Lunch? Rice*, Franklin Watts

*Body Works: Eating*, Paul Bennett, Belitha

# INDEX

# Titles in the *Food* series include:

Hardback     0 431 12708 5

Hardback     0 431 12700 X

Hardback     0 431 12702 6

Hardback     0 431 12706 9

Hardback     0 431 12701 8

Hardback     0 431 12703 4

Hardback     0 431 12707 7

Hardback     0 431 12705 0

Find out about the other titles in this series on our website www.heinemann.co.uk/library